D1128495

3 8749 0060 1840 2

GRAPHIC GREEK MYTHS AND LEGENDS

ODYSSEUS

AND THE CYCLOPS

By Gilly Cameron Cooper

Consultant: Dr. Nick Saunders,
University College London

WORLD ALMANAC® LIBRARY

Please visit our web site at: www.garethstevens.com
For a free color catalog describing World Almanac® Library's list of high-quality books and multimedia programs, call 1-800-848-2928 (USA) or 1-800-387-3178 (Canada). World Almanac® Library's fax: (414) 332-3567.

Library of Congress Cataloging-in-Publication Data available upon request from publisher. Fax (414) 336-0157 for the attention of the Publishing Records Department.

ISBN-13: 978-0-8368-7746-5 (lib. bdg.)
ISBN-13: 978-0-8368-8146-2 (softcover)

This North America edition first published in 2007 by
World Almanac® Library
A Member of the WRC Media Family of Companies
330 West Olive Street, Suite 100
Milwaukee, WI 53212 USA

Illustrators: Bookmatrix

World Almanac® Library managing editor: Valerie J. Weber
World Almanac® Library art direction: Tammy West

Printed in Canada

1 2 3 4 5 6 7 8 9 10 10 09 08 07 06

CONTENTS

THE GREEKS, THEIR GODS, & MYTHS

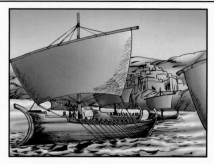

The world of the ancient Greeks was bound by the Mediterranean Sea and the rugged lands surrounding it. It was a place of dangerous winds and sudden storms. The ancient Greeks saw their lives as controlled by spirits of nature and the gods. They told myths about how the gods fought with each other and created the universe. These stories helped explain what caused natural events, such as lightning and earthquakes, and the fates of individuals.

The ancient Greeks believed that 12 gods and goddesses ruled over the world. The 10 gods and goddesses shown on the next page are the most important ones. Some of them appear in this myth.

The ancient Greek gods and goddesses looked and acted like human beings. They fell in love, were jealous and vain, and argued with each other. But unlike humans, they were immortal. They did not die but lived forever. They also had superhuman strength and specific magical powers. Each god or goddess controlled certain forces of nature or aspects of human life, such as marriage or hunting.

In the myths, the gods had their favorite humans. Sometimes, the gods even had children with these people. Their children were thus half gods. They were usually mortal, which meant that they could die. It also meant that they had some special powers, too. When their human children were in trouble, the gods would help them.

The gods liked to meddle in human life and took sides with different people. The gods also liked to play tricks on humans. They did so for many reasons—because it was fun; because they would gain something; or because they wanted to get even with someone.

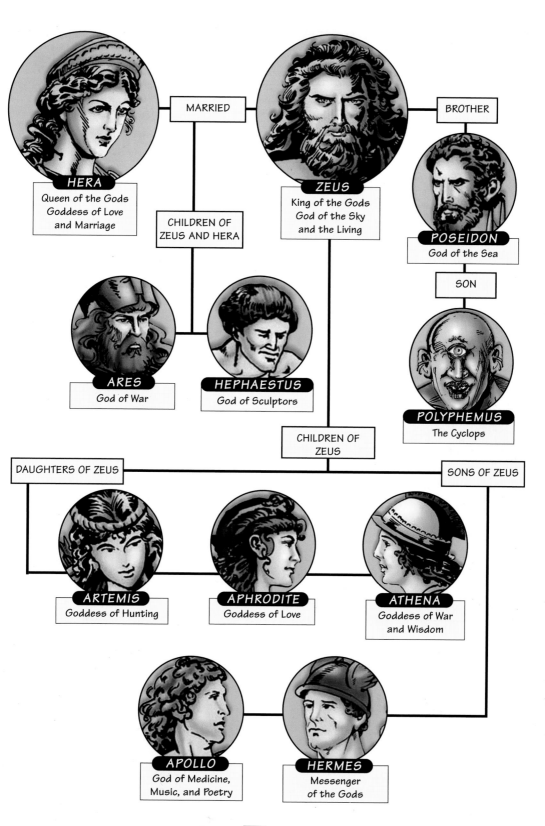

HERA
Queen of the Gods
Goddess of Love
and Marriage

MARRIED

ZEUS
King of the Gods
God of the Sky
and the Living

BROTHER

POSEIDON
God of the Sea

SON

CHILDREN OF
ZEUS AND HERA

ARES
God of War

HEPHAESTUS
God of Sculptors

POLYPHEMUS
The Cyclops

CHILDREN OF
ZEUS

DAUGHTERS OF ZEUS

SONS OF ZEUS

ARTEMIS
Goddess of Hunting

APHRODITE
Goddess of Love

ATHENA
Goddess of War
and Wisdom

APOLLO
God of Medicine,
Music, and Poetry

HERMES
Messenger
of the Gods

HOW THE MYTH BEGINS

This myth begins at the end of the Trojan War. The war had started because Paris of Troy had fled for home with the King of Sparta's wife, Helen. Odysseus and other Greek warriors sailed off to Troy to get Helen back. The resulting war lasted 10 years. The gods helped the Greeks win the Trojan War and destroy the city of Troy. But Odysseus and his warriors had killed many men, so the gods decided that they should be punished. Their punishment was to suffer a long and dangerous journey home to Ithaca. Many times along the way, Odysseus and his men almost lost their lives. They also met many strange creatures, including a sorceress and a one-eyed giant—the cyclops.

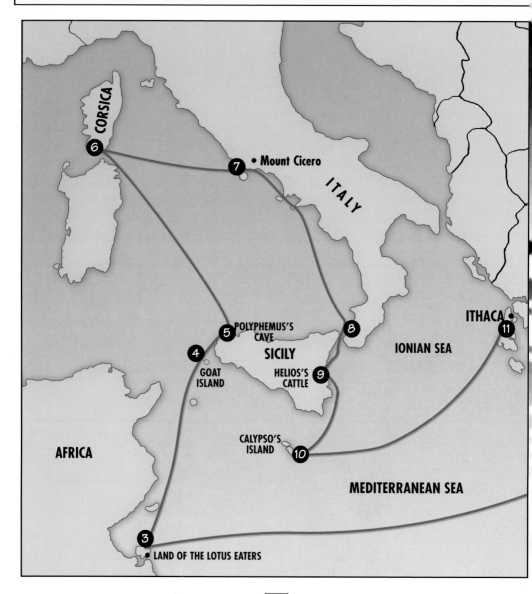

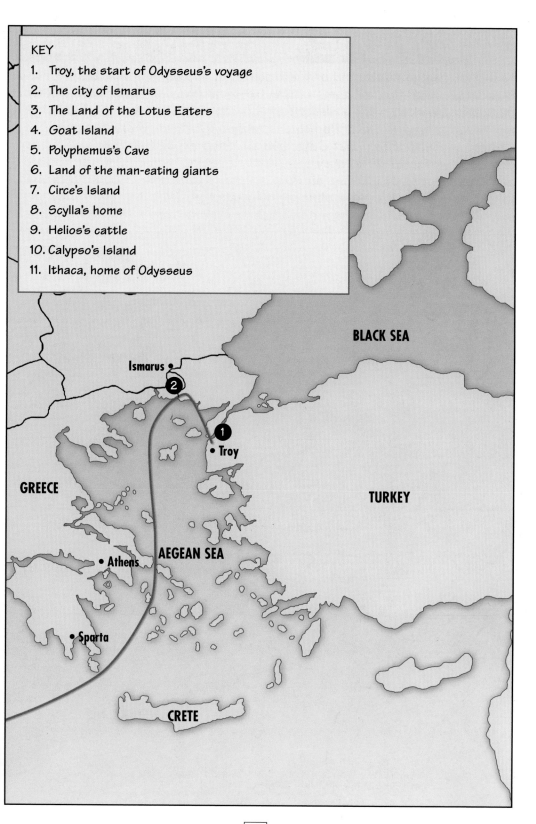

KEY

1. Troy, the start of Odysseus's voyage
2. The city of Ismarus
3. The Land of the Lotus Eaters
4. Goat Island
5. Polyphemus's Cave
6. Land of the man-eating giants
7. Circe's Island
8. Scylla's home
9. Helios's cattle
10. Calypso's Island
11. Ithaca, home of Odysseus

BLACK SEA

Ismarus

Troy

GREECE

TURKEY

AEGEAN SEA

Athens

Sparta

CRETE

A LONG WAY FROM HOME

After 10 years of fighting, Odysseus and his men wanted to go home to their island of Ithaca. But many years before the war, a priestess had given Odysseus a message from the gods: "Fight in the Trojan War, and you will not return home for 20 years." Odysseus wondered, "What dangers and adventures could make our journey last so long? Would the gods be on our side, as they had been during the wars?"

Ithaca lay southwest of Troy. But Zeus, king of the gods and master of the sky, sent a wind to drive the fleet north.

Forced north, the fleet reached the city of Ismarus. Odysseus and his men thought greedily about the food and treasure that they might find there. They decided to sack the city.

It's not time for you to go home yet, Odysseus.

The people of Ismarus were caught by surprise. Odysseus and his warriors showed no mercy, killing all the men of fighting age. They took the women and children as slaves.

We'll be feasting tonight!

There's some rich pickings here.

Run!

Near the city, the Greek warriors found Maro, priest of Apollo. Wisely, Odysseus spared him and his son. With the gods already against them, he couldn't risk upsetting Apollo. Maro thanked him with presents that would prove useful later.

Odysseus's men piled up the treasure that they had stolen.

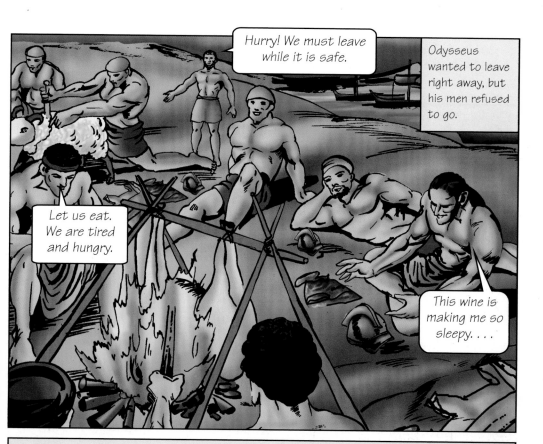

They slept heavily after their feast. At dawn, a deadly attack of spears awoke them. The people from around Ismarus wanted revenge for Odysseus's attack. During the battle, six men from each ship were killed before the fleet could escape.

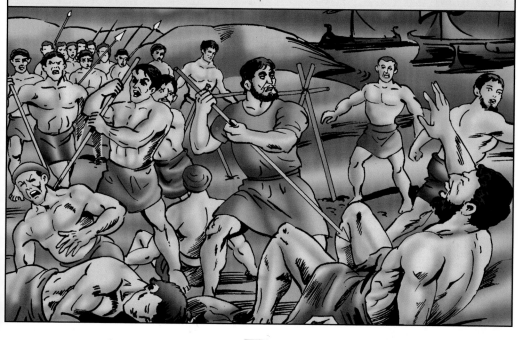

Eventually, the storm passed by. But then Zeus sent the ships in the direction of an island. Desperate for fresh water, Odysseus sent three men to find some.

The islanders were friendly and offered the three warriors bowls of lotus fruit. The fruit was as sweet as honey, making them relaxed and happy . . . and forget about Odysseus.

Odysseus went in search of his men. When he found them, Odysseus realized the lotus fruit had put them under a spell. He dragged them back to the ships.

A PROMISING LAND

Odysseus and his fleet sailed on. They wondered what horrors Zeus and the other gods might be planning for them. One night, a heavy mist crept over them, like a black blanket, until they could not see. The lead ships tossed on the rolling waters. The lookouts struggled to guide the ships safely. With hidden rocks all around, they soon ran aground.

As the morning cleared, Odysseus and his men found themselves in a beautiful harbor.

At last, the gods are being kind. My men can rest here.

After resting, they set off to hunt for food. The little wooded island had no signs of human life. There were only goats, hundreds of them, unafraid of humans. . . .

Look, there's another . . . and another. They're everywhere! We'll eat well tonight.

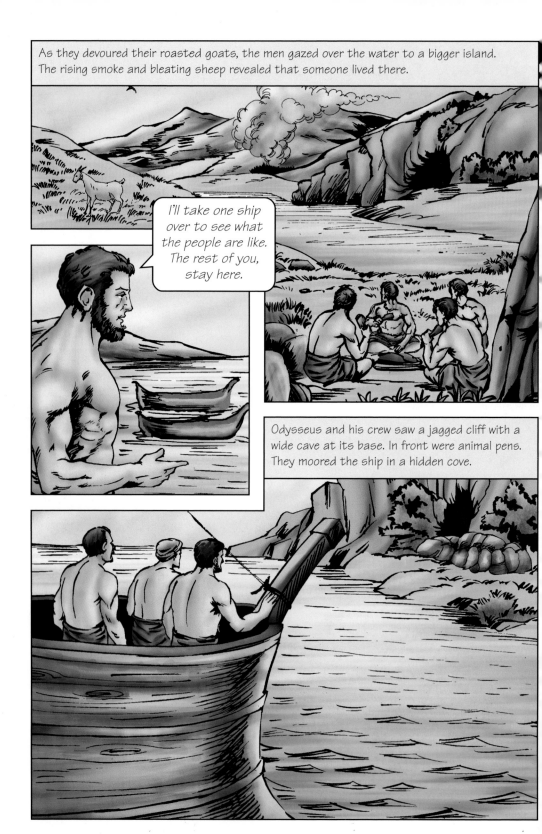

As they devoured their roasted goats, the men gazed over the water to a bigger island. The rising smoke and bleating sheep revealed that someone lived there.

I'll take one ship over to see what the people are like. The rest of you, stay here.

Odysseus and his crew saw a jagged cliff with a wide cave at its base. In front were animal pens. They moored the ship in a hidden cove.

16

What sort of creature lived in the huge cave? Odysseus picked 12 of his bravest and strongest men to go with him. They scrambled over boulders to reach the cave's entrance.

There was no one at home. The animal pen was made of huge rocks. It must have taken someone very large and strong to lift them.

The men crept into the cave to find baskets of cheese, buckets of milk, and more animals in pens. The men wanted to steal some food and then return to the ship. Odysseus, however, insisted that they stay to find out who lived there. After all, the gods ruled that guests—invited or not—must be treated well. So they waited, cooking some lambs to eat.

Suddenly, heavy footsteps shook the cave. The hideous bulk of a giant, Polyphemus, filled the entrance. A single bulging eye moved in the center of his forehead. He didn't notice the humans.

I'm so tired of eating nothing but goat meat.

Oh, no, it's a cyclops! They hate humans!

Polyphemus lit a fire before picking up an massive slab of stone that he used as a door. He placed it over the cave entrance. It was so big that 20 oxen could not have moved it. As he turned, he caught sight of his visitors in the flickering firelight.

Odysseus's heart sank into his sandals as he faced the cyclops. He bravely explained that they had been driven off course as they returned home from Troy.

Don't forget, the gods punish those who do not welcome travelers.

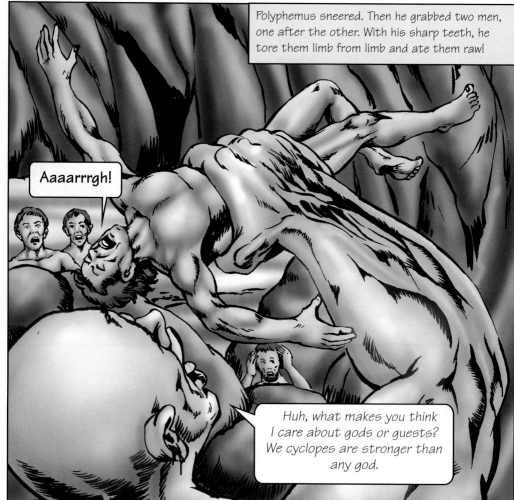

Polyphemus sneered. Then he grabbed two men, one after the other. With his sharp teeth, he tore them limb from limb and ate them raw!

Aaaarrrgh!

Huh, what makes you think I care about gods or guests? We cyclopes are stronger than any god.

Polyphemus lay down on his bed, closed his eye, and soon was snoring loudly. Odysseus and his men could do nothing but pray to Zeus. Even if they killed the cyclops, they could never move the great rock blocking the cave entrance.

Show us mercy, oh great gods! Help us find a way out of here.

Zzzzzzzzzzz

Finally, beams of morning light squeezed through the cracks around the giant slab.

Breakfast! I'm thirsty for a big bucket of milk — then for some food.

Polyphemus's huge hand reached out and grabbed another two men.

Crunch

Then, Polyphemus lifted the great stone from the entrance. He stepped into the morning sunlight, his flock walking in front of him. For a moment, Odysseus and his men saw the glittering blue sea and freedom . . .

... but the cyclops turned to slip the boulder back in place. Once again, they were trapped in darkness.

He'll eat us one by one!

I must come up with a plan to get us out of here . . . before we are all eaten alive!

Odysseus set his men to work. Some restarted the cyclops's fire. Others found a tree trunk and used their daggers to shave one end to a point.

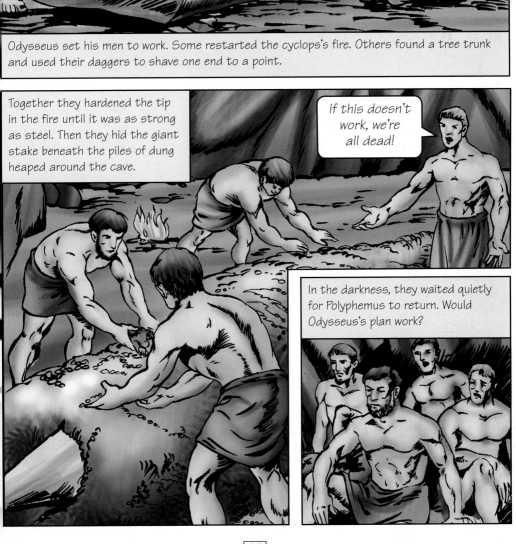

Together they hardened the tip in the fire until it was as strong as steel. Then they hid the giant stake beneath the piles of dung heaped around the cave.

If this doesn't work, we're all dead!

In the darkness, they waited quietly for Polyphemus to return. Would Odysseus's plan work?

TRICKING THE CYCLOPS

Evening fell and Polyphemus finally returned. He herded his animals into the cave and put back the stone at the entrance. Odysseus felt sick when the cyclops grabbed and ate two more of his men. It was time to start the plan.

Polyphemus greedily gulped the wine and demanded more. Three bowls later, he was drunk and started talking. When asked his name, clever Odysseus told the cyclops his name was "Odeia" . . . which meant "nobody."

My nickname is Odeia.

Well, Odeia, I have a special treat for you . . . **ha, ha, ha.**

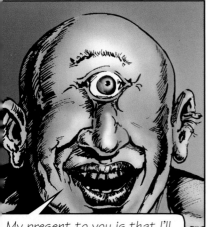

My present to you is that I'll eat you last . . . very slowly . . . **ha, ha, ha!**

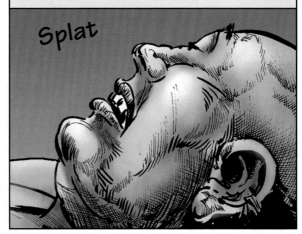

With those words, the drunken cyclops fell over, unconscious. Odysseus's plan was working.

Splat

Quickly, the men grabbed the stake. They laid the point in the cyclops's fire until it glowed red-hot.

Odysseus and his remaining men picked it up. Holding it firmly, they charged at the sleeping cyclops. They rammed the sizzling point into his eye.

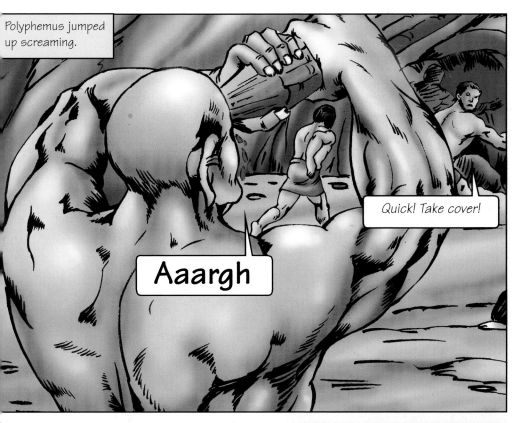

Polyphemus jumped up screaming.

Aaargh

Quick! Take cover!

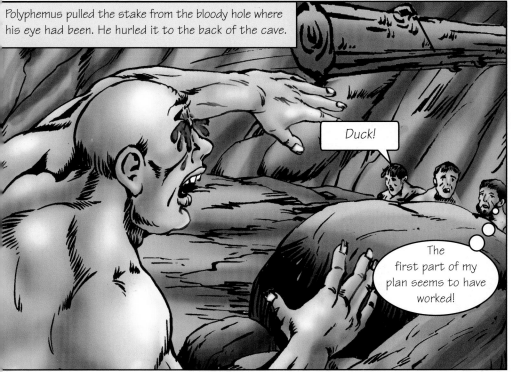

Polyphemus pulled the stake from the bloody hole where his eye had been. He hurled it to the back of the cave.

Duck!

The first part of my plan seems to have worked!

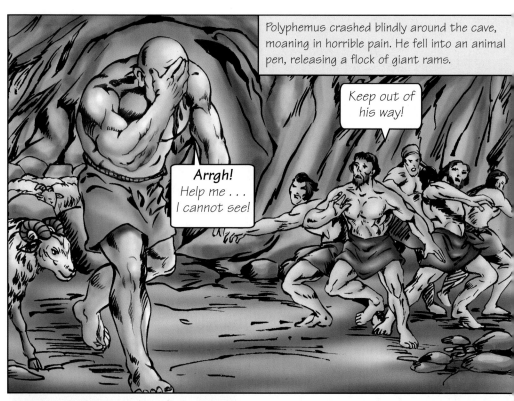

Polyphemus crashed blindly around the cave, moaning in horrible pain. He fell into an animal pen, releasing a flock of giant rams.

Keep out of his way!

Arrgh! Help me . . . I cannot see!

Outside, other cyclopes came running from nearby caves. What was Polyphemus yelling about?

You've woken us up!

It's Polyphemus shouting.

Is something attacking him?

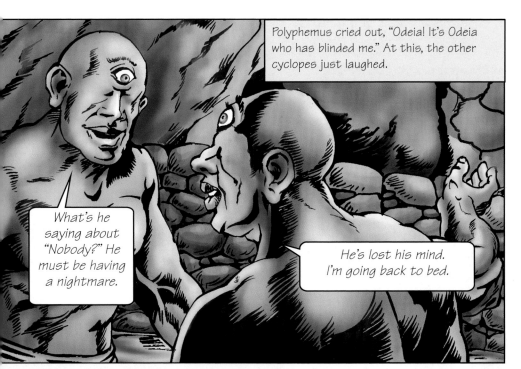

Polyphemus cried out, "Odeia! It's Odeia who has blinded me." At this, the other cyclopes just laughed.

What's he saying about "Nobody?" He must be having a nightmare.

He's lost his mind. I'm going back to bed.

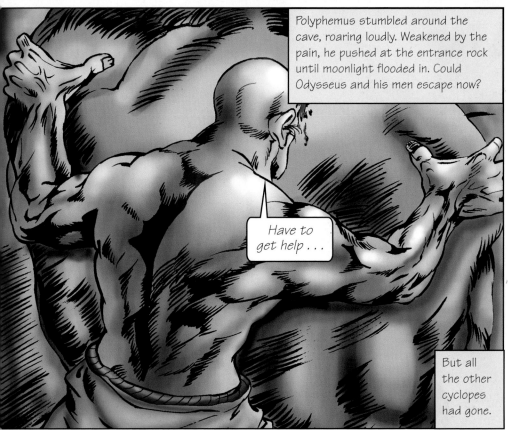

Polyphemus stumbled around the cave, roaring loudly. Weakened by the pain, he pushed at the entrance rock until moonlight flooded in. Could Odysseus and his men escape now?

Have to get help . . .

But all the other cyclopes had gone.

BLIND MAN'S BLUFF

In the moonlight, Polyphemus plopped down in front of the cave entrance groaning quietly in pain. He blocked the light—and Odysseus's hope of escape. The cyclops's huge hands swept the ground around him, checking, making sure no human could slip past him.

Odysseus racked his brains for some way to get around the cyclops. He remembered the branches that made up Polyphemus's bed . . . and the big, fleecy rams.

Mmmm, maybe that will work. . . . Men, pray to Zeus for his help! I have an idea.

Odysseus leapt into action, driven by hope. He caught three of the big rams and tied them together with the branches.

I must work quickly before the other cyclopes wake up and realize what is happening.

Odysseus tied together five more ram teams. Finally, there was one team for each of his surviving men. Each warrior slid under the middle ram in his team, and Odysseus strapped his men in.

For himself, Odysseus took the biggest ram of all. He squeezed himself under its belly and held on to the thick fleece for dear life.

As the Sun rose, the rams walked to the mouth of the cave, ready to go to the fields. As they passed Polyphemus, the cyclops ran his hands over their backs. He wanted to make sure that no one was riding them. Soon, all the rams were out in the open. Only the biggest ram, the one carrying Odysseus, remained.

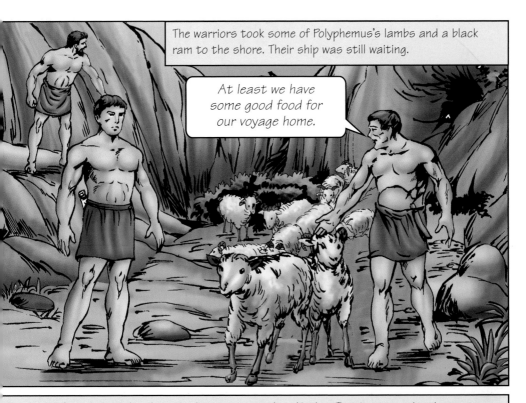

The warriors took some of Polyphemus's lambs and a black ram to the shore. Their ship was still waiting.

At least we have some good food for our voyage home.

The men left guarding the ship were happy to see their leader. Their joy turned to horror as they realized that half of the returning group was missing. There was no time to explain.

Where are the others?

What are you talking about?

Dead? Eaten alive?

Hurry! I'll tell you later. Get the animals on the ship and let's go!

PARTING SHOTS

Odysseus and his men were on their way to safety. The men rowed fast, and a breeze soon caught the sails. The ship sliced quickly through the waves. Odysseus saw Polyphemus stumble onto the cliffs behind them.

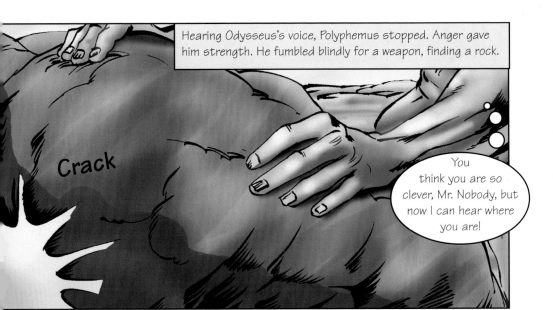

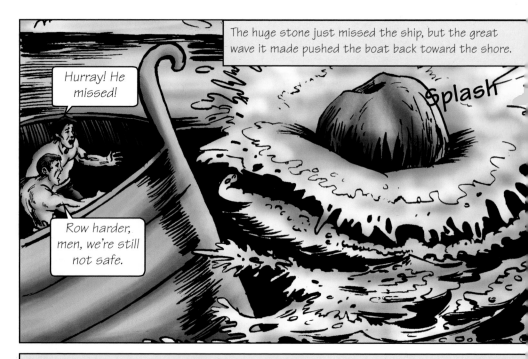

The huge stone just missed the ship, but the great wave it made pushed the boat back toward the shore.

Hurray! He missed!

Row harder, men, we're still not safe.

Splash

Just in time, Odysseus steered the ship away before it could crash. Despite the danger, he started to taunt the cyclops.

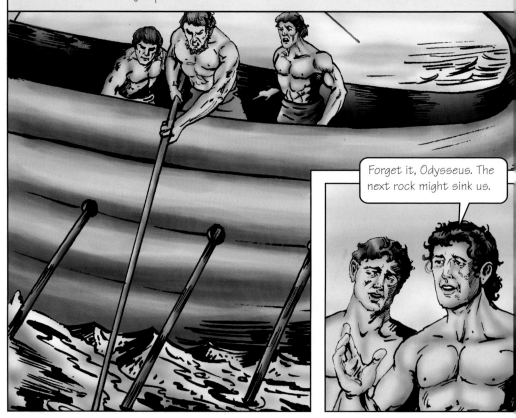

Forget it, Odysseus. The next rock might sink us.

Polyphemus was furious. He raised himself to his full, ugly height. He called to his father, the great god Poseidon, for help.

Father of the Seas, help me! Odysseus and his fleet must never reach Ithaca.

Poseidon knew Zeus and the other gods were angry with Odysseus .

Odysseus has gone against us too many times.

Polyphemus grabbed an even bigger rock and threw it at the ship.

Again the rock missed, this time washing the boat out to sea and to safety.

Back on the first island, Odysseus and his entire fleet ate the cyclops's sheep and drank wine. They thanked the gods for their safety. Odysseus sacrificed the big black ram, offering it to Zeus in return for a safe voyage back to Ithaca.

POSEIDON'S REVENGE

It was soon obvious that Odysseus's sacrifice and prayers were not enough. Zeus could see no reason to change his mind. The travelers' journey would continue to be long, hard, and dangerous. Now that Odysseus had also annoyed Poseidon by blinding his son, more danger would come their way.

First, on the island of Corsica, man-eating giants killed many of Odysseus's warriors. Only Odysseus and his ship's crew escaped.

After this lucky escape, the men took to the seas. But soon Circe, a beautiful sorceress, lured them to her island and turned them into pigs. Odysseus's charm finally convinced her to make them men again.

Surely you would rather have men than pigs?

They also dodged deadly whirlpools. But then, the six-headed monster, Scylla, ate six of Odysseus's crew. Worse, though, was yet to come. . . .

Odyssus and his men then becme trapped on Helios's island. This god did not allow anyone to eat his cattle. But as the days passed, the men's food supply shrank. Finally, the men ate some cows. Odysseus, who had not eaten, rushed his men to their ships. An angry Helios complained to Zeus. The god of the sky raised a terrible storm when Odysseus and his men were back at sea. The last ship was destroyed, and one by one, the rest of Odysseus's crew died.

It angers me to spare you, Odysseus, but since you did not eat the meat, I cannot punish you.

Odysseus was left on his own. Clinging to a a piece of wood, he drifted to the goddess Calypso's land. Calypso kept Odysseus as a prisoner for seven years, despite his pleas to go home to Ithaca. Eventually, the other gods felt sorry for Odysseus and persuaded Calypso to let Odysseus go.

Odysseus arrived home to find his lovely wife, Penelope, waiting for him and his son, Telemachus, who had grown up. Having battled countless monsters for 10 years, the gods finally agreed that Odysseus had paid his price for fighting in the Trojan War. He lived many happy years on Ithaca.

GLOSSARY

Circe *a Greek sorceress who could turn men into animals*

cove *a small bay on a coastline*

Cyclopes: *nasty, one-eyed giants*

dung *manure*

fleece *a sheep's wool coat*

fleet *a group of ships*

herd *to gather into a group*

lotus fruit *a mythical fruit that makes people relax and forget things*

mercy *forgiveness or care*

moor *to park a ship*

myths *the stories of a tribe or people that tell of their gods, heroes, and turning points in their history*

pen *a place where animals are kept together, usually surrounded by a fence or wall*

priest/priestess *a man or woman who devotes his or her life to serving a god or gods*

ram *a male sheep*

revenge *to get even for something done wrong to a person*

sack *to attack, destroy, and loot a city or building*

sacrifice *an offering, such as a specially killed animal, to a god in the hope of winning the god's support*

Scylla *a six-headed female monster who lived in the Straits of Messina between the southern tip of Italy and Sicily. If sailors escaped the whirlpool of Charybdis on the other side of the channel, they fell into the deadly clutches of Scylla.*

sorceress *a woman who can do magic and use spells to control other people*

spare *to let someone go without hurting them*

Trojan War *the war of all the Greek kingdoms against the city-state of Troy. It began when Helen, the most beautiful woman in the ancient world, left her Spartan husband, Menelaus, for Paris, prince of Troy. Odysseus and his men were one of the Greek forces to fight at Troy. The war lasted 10 years before the Greeks finally won.*

Troy *the city-state where the Trojan Wars were fought*

unconscious *unaware of one's self or one's surroundings; knocked out or asleep*

BOOKS

Homer, and Adrian Mitchell. *The Odyssey*. Dorling Kindersley Classics (series). New York: DK Children, 2000.

Lupton, Hugh. *The Adventures of Odysseus*. Cambridge, MA: Barefoot Books, 2006.

Osborne, Mary Pope. *The One-Eyed Giant*. Tales from the Odyssey: Book #1 (series). New York: Hyperion, 2003.

Reid, Sue, and David Salariya. *The Voyages of Odysseus*. Ancient Myths (series). Minneapolis, MN: Picture Window Books, 2004.

Sutcliff, Rosemary. *The Wanderings of Odysseus: The Story of the Odyssey*. New York: Laurel-Leaf Books, 2005.

WEB SITES

Mythweb

www.mythweb.com/encyc/entries/ odysseus.html
Read another story about Odysseus's fight with the Cyclops and his adventures on his way home to Ithaca.

Odysseus

www.mythweb.com/odyssey
Find short or detailed versions of the twenty books of the Odyssey with illustrations on this site.

Winged Sandals

www.abc.net.au/arts/wingedsandals
Learn about Odysseus and other Greek heroes, gods, and myths as you tour this Web site.

Publisher's note to educators and parents: Our editors have carefully reviewed these Web sites to ensure that they are suitable for children. Many Web sites change frequently, however, and we cannot guarantee that a site's future contents will continue to meet our high standards of quality and educational value. Be advised that children should be closely supervised whenever they access the Internet.

INDEX